Giancarlo Gasponi

# ROME REVEALED

Introduction
Enzo Siciliano

Text by
Livio Jannattoni

art assistant
Rouhyeh Avaregan

Editoria - Trento

Rome, a city both Levantine and Mediterranean; Rome, gateway to the Orient, entrance to a world woven inextricably of corruption and the morals of the market place. One has read a great deal and there is much more still to read. Rome, the embodiment of all Italian vices. There are times when the whole country disgorges upon the capital every kind of hardship: instead of seeing in it the reflection and encapsulation of its own sorry plight, it is regarded as the cause of it, as if a city, of its own accord, by the force of its own spirit, could produce such general malaise and perversity.

Rome, indolent and drowsy, but also cruel, was, as the poet Belli shows, from the time of Unification onwards, occupied by people from all over Italy, who poured into it as much as they could compress of tertiary and parasitic activities. The mischief and the damage both to the city itself and to the nation of which it was elected capital, began here, from that progressive occupation, ever accelerating under fascism and the aftermath of the Second World War. By reading the first «parliamentary» novels, *Daniele Curtis* by Fogazzaro or *The Empire* by De Roberto, one sees clearly how much Rome has always limited itself to the role of a spectator, a host to the plots, the trafficking, more or less illicit, of men of power come up from the most distant provinces.

To such plots, to such trafficking, to such scandals, the city afforded the refuge or shelter of its cynical tolerance, its laugh perhaps soured by a bitterness long nurtured by its history. Rome as she once was, and in part still is, watched: in the way she had watched till then the succession of the many popes to the «Palazzo».[1] If there is an unbroken thread in the city's vicissitudes over the centuries, it is here in its divided being: on the one hand the spirit of the populace, a spirit that brought together princes and grocers, vineyard labourers and clergy, all speaking the same dialect; on the other, the spirit of the Curia or the «Palazzo». This Pasolini-like image, now in common use, is without doubt derived from Belli, who used it to symbolise the source of Apostolic authority – with its secrets, its intrigues and its machinations – a distant place to be viewed with indifference and disdain. Even to enter it was to say the least, difficult.

«Tu vvà a le cchiese de Palazzo: vacce
E, ssi nun entri pe la gattarola,
Vatte a ttrovà la porta per entracce.»

«Go to the church of the Palazzo: go on:
And, if you can't get in by the back door,
Go and find the main entrance.»

Or (and this sonnet seems to sum up and project «ad eternum» the Italian, Roman Catholic conception of power):

«Tutti quanti a Palazzo lo vederno.
Un gran Ministro d'un gran Potenza
Venne a Rroma a pparlà cco Ssu'Eminenza
Er Zegretar-de-Stato de l'isterno.
    Er Cardinale preparò un quinterno
De carta bianca, e ppoi je diede udienza;
E cce tenne un gran circonferenza
Sopra a ttutti l'affari der governo.
    Tra llòro se trattò dder più e der meno;
E scannajjorno l'ummido e l'asciutto,
Er callo e 'r freddo, er nuvolo e 'r zereno.
    Arfine er Cardinale uprì la porta,
Discenno: "Evviva, è ccombinato tutto:
Ne parleremo mejjo un'artra vorta".»


Come to Rome to talk with his Eminence
The Secretary of State for Foreign Affairs.
    The Cardinal prepared reams
Of blank paper and then gave audience;
And a grand conference was held,

Above all about affairs of state.
    They got down to business about this and that;
And the daily forecast of the wet and the dry,
The hot and the cold, the cloudy and the clear.
    In the end the Cardinal opened the door
Saying: "Splendid, it's all settled:
We'll talk about it again another time".»

The will of the «Palazzo» against the will of the people; but it is the former which, capable of the most outragious subterfuges, has made shrewd use of the fact that the unified country has deemed fit to send it its emissaries. Can it be said, however, that this Roman Catholic spirit is «Roman» in the fullest sense of the word? The answer to this question has filled whole sections of libraries and has led to the liveliest controversies. As far as I am concerned, I believe that the Roman «Palazzo» was born of a gathering together of multifarious events on a national scale in which the city itself played a limited part. One knows that a cardinal born in Rome, once the triple crowned mitre is on his head, remains Roman only in name: being Pope, even if it is a pope like Belli's «Gregoriaccio» (Gregory the Bad), was a question of «urbis», but much more, and disconcertingly so, of «orbis».
This city, then, because of its particular nature, is to be examined differently and looked at in a different light. Its cupolas, its churches, as well as its princely palaces (princes, moreover, sprung from shepherds and goatherds, cheese–makers, cow–hands, land–robbers, and not princes of the Holy Roman Empire: as Stendhal noted) should not be confused with the other «Palazzo» and its history.
«Rome Revealed» is the title of this volume of photographs by Giancarlo Gasponi. Leafing through the photographs which compose it and cover a historical span of time, one can clearly see how Gasponi went about

with his camera in search of that «other» Rome, that secret Rome, that neither polemics nor architectural and urban monstrosities have suppressed. I said a secret Rome: I should have said the particular atmosphere of the city that one can still breathe secretly at certain hours of the day and night, when there is a sudden change of season, a sudden downpour, or when the sun shines unexpectedly. This is the atmosphere of the Rome of the common people that I distinguished from the atmosphere of the «Palazzo». Brawlers, young boys, light–fingered and handy with a knife; women seemingly sacrificed to lives of infamy: such as the pregnant whore whom Caravaggio used as a model for the dead Virgin (the woman is said to have drowned in the Tiber); or again all those nuns named Costanza and others whom Belli put into his two thousand sonnets: in short the Roman people seem destined to a savage fate, a life of torment and grief. Already in the fourteenth century the climate was no different, as is revealed in the chronicle of an anonymous writer describing the lynching of Cola di Rienzo. One could say that the city was enfolded in a «scirocco» that unsettles the blood and leads to disaster, confusion, and the blunting of finer feelings.

Except for the «ponentino»,[1] the scirocco is the city's true wind, a continual repetition of alternating hot gusts and icy blasts.

That this is so is a fact, but facts are made up of contradictions, or rather are fed by contradictions. Looked at closely, Rome betrays a sad hollowness set against a background of ruins, baroque facades, splashing fountains, the winding river and avenues heavy with plane trees. Inside there reigns a silence that induces all passions to languish and fade away. The empty Rome that Gasponi allows us to see through the eye of his camera is just this. The blue thistles that cover the

Claudio Acqueduct; the fennel, and the sheep with their shepherd on the Old Appian Way, no different from those the characters in the novel *«Piacere»* saw while out riding, as the sun or the year «very gently died away»: the catmint in Trajan's Market or the ivy and ilex on the Palatine hill; the Colosseum seen from afar as if it were out in the country; the red geranium protruding from a marble window–sill; the naked boy bathing in a fountain near La Bocca della Verità; the faces of the seminarists, eternally the same, expressing that explicit malevolence of ingenuousness; the artichoke–vendor's cart in Campo dei Fiori or the water–melon man at the Pantheon; the old men on the Isola Tiberina (the Tiber Island); the little boy playing hide–and–seek behind a wall; the cobbles in Piazza di Spagna newly polished after rain; the newspaper stall in Vicolo dei Piedi in the close embrace of a creeper; the blacksmith, the knife–grinder, the baker's boy and the shrine–makers..... gulls gliding up river; the sun setting behind the «cupolone» or great dome of St. Peter's.

All the pictures, even those of a rare delicacy, are tainted with the same melancholy sickness – but in the end it is not a sickness; rather it is a philosophy or that distortion of sensibility into a form of restless indecision and solitary suffering which is the very spirit of the Roman people.

The flooding of Piazza Navona on Saturdays and Sundays takes place no more. It was the custom to block the fountains' drain pipes: urchins and patrician carriages would rush back and forth in the lakes which formed round the fountains, looked down upon with gentle gaze by Sant'Agnese who stands forth high up on tle gaze by St. Agnes standing high up on the façade of Borromini's basilica as if striking a melodramatic pose. It was all great fun, an entertainment ancient in origin and a little demented. Neither is the Carnival any longer celebrated in Via del Corso.

Horses would charge headlong from Porta del Popolo, past Palazzo Doria to Palazzo Venezia. That too was a mad caper but also of ancient origin, that inspired many tall stories and desperate battles. Géricault was just in time to paint it, and he did so in the gloomy colours of the slaughter–house.

All this has gone. A way of life has disappeared and all that remains is a tremulous, heart–rending echo.

The «other» Rome. That anarchical, epicurean, non–Christian touch that hides tenaciously under the narcissistic bombast, the unshakeable adolescent exhibitionism of the Roman populace (meaning, I repeat, all Romans), has its clear reverse side in a certain gloominess, and in a breath of sensuality deriving from a twisted misanthropy. All this, in Anno Domini 1981, has not disappeared – it seems a miracle. Such is the empty Rome through which Gasponi, with his bewitching pictures, leads us. Only the summer light, certain noonday flashes of lightning which empty the most crowded piazzas; only the biting gusts of the «tramontana» (north wind) seem to give a vibrant reality to this city of ghosts.

It is thus the portrait of a city that has survived, that Gasponi has lovingly rediscovered and painted in these pages. The raindrops have a special bond with the old streets, the light falls lazily but not without curiosity on the lined faces of the old women sitting on their doorsteps; a slow stupor imbues everything with a calm and listless companionship, endowing an equal venerability to old marble, old towers, old cupolas, old cats, old carts, old priests and beardless youths with the croaky voices of old age.

ENZO SICILIANO

---

[1] «Palazzo» as used here means the Vatican, seat of the highest authority of the Church and for many centuries, of course, also the centre of temporal power in Rome.

---

[1] Ponentino – The gentle little evening breeze from the west.

# OUTSIDE THE WALLS:
# THE RUINS
# AND THE COUNTRYSIDE

A Rome, outside the walls, or on the edge of the boundary, that Gasponi has preferred to capture undefiled by modern additions. Purely a free communion between nature and the ruins. But it would be enough merely to raise or lower the camera to catch, with horror, a city in the grip of an urbanistic siege.

In this «isolation» on may still sense that breath of the countryside that one would have thought lost for ever. Standing out against a tapestry of wild flowers we see in the distance the harmoniously suffused image of a ruin, or perhaps we see a flowing stream, or a placidly grazing herd of sheep that is in counterpoint to the arches of the acqueducts, the skeletons of the old villas and the paving stones of the Old Appian Way. There is one particular view that reveals the survival of a spirit that draws us inexorably towards a Rome that was. This is the picture of the sheep spread out along the slope of a hillside whose edge cuts across the bluish outlines of the dome of St. Peter's.

1849, during the Roman Republic, as related in the memoirs of Nino Costa, a great painter and patriot. Rome was besieged by the French. Many of her inhabitants had fled to the hills and were anxious for news from relations and friends left behind. Sometimes they were successful, sometimes not. But it was far easier to learn the latest news from the shepherd boy who grazed his sheep as closely as possible to the city. Thus, to the question, «How goes it in Rome?» the boy could answer with impunity, while evoking the picture precisely, «The shepherd's hut still stands and the shepherd is returning», meaning the Basilica and the exiled Pope respectively.

In a nostalgic vein one could conjure up from this sequence of photographs the festivities of the Romans of yore, and the expeditions «fori porta» (beyond the gates) when the taverns on the edge of the city stood on the threshold of vineyards, and fields of artichokes and broad beans. A primordial, patriarchal way of life that made Rome also the undisputed queen of wine and country fare. Such country views as have fortunately survived, have over the years, here more than most, lost their particular character as distinct places on a map and have acquired that universal appearance and atmosphere of places totally and exclusively Roman. The fortified Ponte Nomentana, for example, arching over the water between the green banks of the lazy river Aniene brings to mind famous historical and literary events: the Villa dei Quintili, whose ruins the passing centuries and lack of care have not yet completely obscured: the Stadio di Massenzio almost like a sea wall for the tomb of Cecilia Metella, encompassing a huge field forming a mystical «bay».

It is hardly surprising that Chateaubriand preferred these places above all others in which to follow his botanical studies. He was the father of all the great eulogists of the Roman Campagna and there is not an artist, poet, or writer who, like him, has not passed here at least once, to seek inspiration among the composite elements of the most illustrious landscape in the world. To this landscape is added the indispensable complement of the sky. «Vous avez sans doute admiré dans les paysages de Claude Lorrain?» asked Chateaubriand of Monsieur de Fontanes, «cette lumière qui semble ideale et plus belle que nature? eh bien, c'est la lumière de Rome!» (No doubt you have admired in the landscapes of Claude Lorrain that light which seems so perfect and more beautiful than nature itself? Well, that is the Roman light!). Ponte Nomentana and the towers of the recently restored Porta Asinaria are linked indissolubly by the similar style and brickwork of the two buildings. Strengthened according to the prevailing canons of military architecture the result is grandiose, but it did not stand up to Totila's Goths. Punishment for this failure came a thousand years later when it was replaced in its ancient office by the Renaissance Porta S. Giovanni. Yet it still continues to frame in harmonious contrast as seen from a particular view point the brilliance of the Travertine marble and the enormous gesticulating statues on the façade of the Lateran Basilica. Then there is the Tomb of the Scipioni, a monument that presents an archeological enigma at least for the layman, and is pre–Christian dating back to the heroic Republican era. All Europe was excited when it was brought to light at the end of the 18th century. Thanks, above all, to Count Alessandro Verri who put into words the sense of the melancholy of ruins in his book, «Roman Nights» which was directly inspired by this remarkable discovery.

At the opposite pole, all solidity and simplicity of line stands the Arch of Druso which, a few metres away from that famous tomb, still seems to bar our entrance, in the same way that it once controlled the flow of the crowds intent upon passing through the gateway to reach the Old Appian Way. Called simply «l'arco», this arch is an imposing and rudimentary structure ennobled by the key–stone which constitutes the authentic and absolute seal of Rome's architectural glory.

At the Porta San Paolo we find more towers and more brickwork. The «brick red» which is the basic colour of Rome. And the pyramid of Caius Cestius, built according to the inscription, to the glory and memory of that rich voluptuary in only 330 days. These are monuments that have looked upon the greater part of Roman history right up to the 10th September 1943 when soldiers and citizens together in common accord, opposed the German troops in desperate and heroic resistance.

In the foreground the Pyramid is facing, almost protectively overlooking, the oldest part of the Protestant cemetery also called the Non–Catholic or English Cemetery. This cemetery lies just inside the city walls. In the beginning, however, when the decision to use this plot of land for this melancholy purpose could be reached only by means of considerable diplomatic wrangling, it was so far from any other buildings as to be considered truly outside the walls. It was the same in the case of the Prati del Popolo Romano (the neighbouring Roman People's Fields), which were also separated from the edge of the Campagna only by the shield of that ancient bastion.

There is clear reason for recalling such a romantic place. John Keats is buried there in that little plot and further along almost as far as the towers on the Aurelian Walls Percy Bysshe Shelley is buried. His death, in 1822, was but a year after that of his friend. A very short lifetime, but long enough, however, for him to write «Adonais», «an elegy on the death of John Keats, author of Endymion, Hyperion etc.». Thus it is the poet himself and his poem, that in honour of another poet and his work serve to consecrate that place and the human and august memories of those buried there.

«John Keats», writes Shelley in the Preface: «died in Rome of consumption, in his twenty–fourth year on the 23rd February 1821; and was buried in the romantic and lonely Protestant cemetery in that city under the pyramid, which is the tomb of Cestius, and the massy wall and towers, now moulding and desolate, which formed the circuit of ancient Rome. The cemetery is an open space among the ruins, covered in winter with violets and daisies. It might make one fall in love with death to think that one should be buried in so sweet a place». In the Middle Ages when a restless and impassioned tendency to symbolism renewed an interest in heraldry and coinage, giving grotesque and animals forms to inanimate objects, Rome was obliged to adopt the lion as its emblem. Onarius of Autun, a 12th. century ecclesiastical writer made this clear with these words, in the newly vulgarized tongue, «Era usanza degli antiqui, che edificavano le cittade a similitudine de beste, e cussi era de ciascuna. Sì che Roma fu edificata a similitudine de lione, in per quello che il lione quasi, sì come Re è sopra le altre beste, così è Roma capo di tucta Italia». (It was the practice of the ancients to symbolize each of their city states by a beast, thus Rome was allotted the lion, because the lion was the king of all animals, just as Rome was the head of Italy). In fact there is a fascinating map in which the figure of a lion, symbol of the Ghibelline faction, struts with its tail uplifted and its jaws open, while the outline of the beast follows the perimeter wall of the city of Rome with its many towers and battlements.

Eight hundred years have gone by since then and Rome has quite clearly gone beyond these emblematic confines. This can best be seen from the air, from whence one's gaze can embrace the whole city; the winding ribbon of the Tiber, the green patches of the villas and gardens, the tree–lined avenues, terracotta rooftops, leaden domes, and glistening white Travertine. Once on the ground, in close contact and from a different perspective, we see other shapes and colours; Rome's thousands of churches, a historic centre almost intact, the apparently rather tame river, monuments, palaces, fountains, archeological sites, and pedestrian precincts where the noise of the traffic seems muffled, almost repulsed by the centuries. Nowadays the whole city, including the jumbled outskirts, is ringed by the Grande Raccordo Anulare. This is a dual–carriageway road some 70 km long about 12 km from the centre of the city, built to join up the great «consular» roads leading out of Rome. Between the old walls and the Raccordo the suburbs are extremely built–up consequently to reach the countryside one must go beyond the Raccordo. The one great exception is the Old Appian Way in the Caffarella Valley, where there are still verdant green banks along both sides which we have already admired in these outstanding photographs. Such views will become even more accessible, the property of everybody for everyone's enjoyment, when the long awaited Appian Archeological Park is finally created.

# THE FORUMS AND
# THE ANCIENT TEMPLES

As a result of an unfortunate tendency to rhetoric a disservice has been performed to these quintessential Roman scenes, to these ancient ruins, so often have they been viewed in the iniquitous light of a misplaced triumphalism. Ours is not the only literature pervaded by a disconsolate nostalgia for the «ancient grandeur» and «majesty» of the ruins, for the walls and the arches of Rome, for the «mother of dead empires», for Petrarch and Leopardi. Such sentiments were brilliantly aided and abetted by the poet Byron, that incomparable eulogist of ancient monuments. For our part let us try to see these monuments with detachment, without doeful yearnings, as the proud testimony of an earlier age, as the outward expression of a distinct and irreplaceable civilization. Above all, let us enjoy and admire them for their intrinsic beauty, and for the unfulfilled ambitions and suffering of which they speak and which gives a sharper outline to our awareness of them. Break of day in the Forum. A moving sight, at once complex and unitary, of a «vastness» with which little can compare, but also conveying an extraordinary gentleness. In the misty light the Column of Phocas stands clearly defined in the foreground, seemingly backed by the campanile of Santa Francesca Romana high up in the background pierced by the early morning rays, but failing to obscure the topmost walls of the Colosseum. To the left stands the colonnade of the Temple of Antoninus and Faustina and above this the façade of the church of S. Lorenzo in Miranda, as it has burgeoned forth over the years, notwithstanding its confinement within the classical edifice. On rising ground to the right the Arch of Titus appears to serve as a ceremonial gateway to the whole site.

Looking from another vantage point one sees a single arch framing the three columns of the temple of Castor and Pollux, long enshrined as the emblematic symbol of the Rome of that time. Indeed, so often had the columns been studied and admired that Giuseppe Sacconi, architect of the monument erected to the memory of King Victor Emanuel II, had no scruples about reproducing their identical form and style in the columns that are such a prominent feature of his «Victorian» edifice. In a view of one angle of the Forum the whitish reconstructed temple of Vesta and the ascending layers of the Palatine hill reappear through one of the side arches of the other great arch, erected in 203 B.C., immediately below the Capitoline Hill, in honour of Septimius Severus. The teeming bas–reliefs with which the time–worn walls of the column are faced renders almost tangible the events through which this magnificent monument has passed in its long involvement in Roman history. From the scattered marble remains overgrown with laurel and the huge flagstones that pave the Sacred Way, the eye rises above the uneven grass of the Roman Forum to the Palatine Hill. From there one way enjoy a view of the ruins spread out below: arches and temples, the proud, detached presence of the Colosseum, the intricately chiselled attic storey of the Arch of Constantine, the whole set in an unbroken, near miraculous expanse of green. Such is the effect of this green that one feels compelled to follow it to that created artificially in the encaustic [1] wall paintings found in Livia's Villa at Prima Porta. Paintings composed of elegantly entwined branches, fruit, flowers, birds and an azure blue for the sky, that to some extent foreshadow landscape painting. They are now no longer at the Villa having been stripped from the walls and placed for safe–keeping in a room of the Rome National Museum at the Baths of Diocletian. From these sepulchral pillars, these sacred altars dispersed about the Forum it is but a short step, and not only by way of the photographs, to the scene of a different altar, this time consecrated to the god Mithras which respect for another, diverse civilization and religion has left untouched here in the depths of the earth beneath the Upper and Lower Basilicas of S. Clemente. The site is imbued with an atmosphere of extraordinary evocative power, this is a perfectly preserved Mithraeum where ceremonial rites were performed and neophytes were initiated according to the custom of that oriental cult imported from overseas.

Returning to the surface we go on to the Foro Boario and the Bocca della Verità (Mouth of Truth), another archetypal «Roman scene». The proximity of the Tiber, the temples, the churches, the arches and even the late–baroque fountain by Bizzaccheri, have always made this quarter this huge irregular square, one of the «sights». Regrettably urban development has robbed it of its architectural cohesion and thereby lowered its standing. Nevertheless it remains noble in years and above all a hub of local life.

We will return in a later section to the Christian monuments of the area: for the moment it is the pagan ones that are the focus of our interest. The four–sided Arch of Janus and the Arch of the Argentari, covered with delicate stone arabesques, set beside the church of S. Giorgio in Velabro; the circular so–called Temple of Vesta but almost certainly dedicated to Hercules the Victor and which perhaps comes down to us because in the early Middle Ages it was transformed into a Christian Church, first called Santo Stefano delle Carrozze (St. Stephen of the Carriages) and then Santa Maria del Sole (St. Mary of the Sun). The other rectangular temple, said to be dedicated to Fortuna Virile (Virile Fortune) was also taken over and used by the Christians under the name of Santa Maria Egiziaca (St. Mary the Egyptian). All are monuments of ancient origin and the house of Nicola de' Crescenzi qualifies as another. This unique structure, a splendid exemple of the Mediaeval style, contradicts the common belief that this was a dark age. It owes its originality to the closely–packed brickwork, to its decorations, to the friezes and to the long inscription in leonine verse. «Niccolò, padrone di questa casa, non ignorò che vana è la gloria del mondo. A edificarla non tanto lo indusse frivola ambizione, quanto il desiderio di rinnovare la magnificenza di Roma». («Nicholas, owner of this house, was not unaware that the glory of this world is vain. In building it he was impelled not so much by frivolous ambition as by a desire to renew the magnificence of Rome»).

The supreme harmony of the classical style, however, must be sought elsewhere in Agrippa's Pantheon, a sovereign monument to Roman architecture. The huge façade, the (later) inscription on the entablature and the awesome majesty of the interior, are both religious architecture and an architecture that is in itself a religion. The vast dimensions of the dome, the coffered ceiling, the central oculus open to the sun and the rain and the Christian cross taken into the ancient pagan temple–later renamed for its new role, Santa Maria ad Martyres (St. Mary of the Martyrs). Lastly there are the external complementary elements in the shape of the charming fountain and the central obelisk in the piazza outside, clearly having no wish to compete in size and grandeur with the monument handed down to us intact from antiquity.

The Portico of Octavia, again built of brick, evokes, though in a very different tone, remote ages and a diverse way of life. For many long years it was to be found as a frontispiece to the ghetto and even today it is firmly welded to its «rione» (district). Elsewhere on the other hand, ancient and modern continue to submerge and confuse each other, cancelling each other out in a common urban transformation. Thus the Cupola del Santissimo Nome di Maria and the Forum of Nerva appear in juxtaposition and a lighted street lamp seems to stand there to illuminate this evidence of that great «mysterious» element of Rome.

The crowning glory of this period, of this particular heritage from antiquity, is to be found in the statue of Marcus Aurelius placed upon the Capitoline Hill as if it were a secular–artistic centre of gravity. It was moved there to add the final touch to Michelangelo's piazza. From then on it has borne witness to everything that has happened in the city, whether joyful or sad. Even before this the statue was bound up intimately with the life of Rome in that up to the year 1538 it had stood in the Lateran square. It was from there that horse and rider had travelled to establish themselves firmly in the centre of a piazza as yet unfreed from its Mediaeval trappings. Their arrival marked the beginning of that vast enterprise, planned and directed in its entirety by Michelangelo and his successors, which transformed the piazza into the architectural masterpiece which we see today.

Once the statue found itself at the centre of the renowned stellar pavement design it became a revered monument, the autocratic custodian of civic affairs and the authentic gnomon (sun dial) of the Roman «day». Thus year by year it came to be looked upon increasingly as the outward and visible symbol of the reality of Rome, almost surpassing the ancient letters S.P.Q.R. since it was a more readily comprehensible emblem of the city and its inhabitants, of their joys and their sorrows. Indeed, for many years it was a direct witness of, and frequently a protagonist in, those events.

Will it or will it not prove to be made of gold, as is expected? The populace believes, as Belli relates in his sonnet «Campidoglio» that «the bulk of the equestrian statue of Marcus Aurelius is constituted of gold which the effects of the atmosphere are slowly bringing to light. The gold is said to have come from the remains of the gold decorative work left in the better–protected parts of the Colosseum. At such time as it is revealed in its entirety the day of Universal Judgement will be upon us». Meanwhile in January 1981 Marcus Aurelius was unhorsed and, together with his mount, sent away for lengthy restoration.

[1] Encaustic: Having the colours hurned in; an ancient method of painting in melted wax.

# CHRISTIAN ROME

In this «Rome Revealed», striving at all times, almost with religious fervour, to exclude the intrusion of mechanization and other modern ills, with their accompanying convulsions and congestions, the influence of Christianity and the measure of its contribution are seen to great advantage. Its history begins with the founding of Christianity in an underground world in the very bowels of Imperial Rome, the Catacombs. To this day places of homage and veneration, they are one of the most powerful attractions that the city has to offer the visitor. Mile after mile of subterranean passages *(cryptae)* along whose walls stretch interminable rows of tombs *(loculi)* or arched tombs with little altar tables *(arcosoli)*, frequently interspersed with small rooms *(cubicoli)* or larger chambers *(cripte)* as well as complete underground churches, for the most part hewn out directly from the tufa rock. The entrances to the catacombs of the saints Sebastian, Domitilla, Calixtus, Priscilla and many others, are spread out all along the ancient Roman roads.

Once the vast Empire had fallen and been rent apart, the Church took possession of the fallen monuments, reclaiming them and putting them to fresh use in establishing its first churches and basilicas (cathedrals), until such time as Christian art developed a style of its own and began to create artistic masterpieces worthy of comparison with those of classical times.

Rome is filled with churches, indeed has an over–abundance of them, built frequently for personal reasons of pride or for the most ungodly purpose of rivalry. One has only to stop at certain points in the centre of the city, the Renaissance centre, to be able to embrace in a single glance two, three, even four or five churches, all of which have flung heavenwards a veritable forest of campanili or bell–towers, ranging in height from S. Maria Maggiore the tallest to S. Benedetto in Priscinula, the smallest. Moreover, as will be seen later, they have added cupolas to the skyline, those superb architectural creations, complete with all their adjuncts, which are so typical of Rome. There is first the «drum», usually colonnaded, on which rests the «cap» covered by the «lantern». This in turn is surmounted by a «spire» which almost always holds up a «ball», a heraldic device of either a pontiff or a cardinal. Finally comes the cross, from which the prosaic, but very practical, lightning conductor snakes its way down to the ground.

The largest cupola, known as the «cupolone», is, of course, the one designed by Michelangelo for the rebuilt basilica of St. Peter's. Here cupola and church are joined in one indissoluble structure, although it must be said that they deviate considerably from the original plan and the lack of warmth of the present church arouses some yearnings for the old demolished basilica.

«The eighth hill of Rome», as the graceful immensity of Michelangelo's cupola has been called, has always exerted an extraordinary fascination. Friedrich Schiller, although he never saw it, sang its praises in just two verses in his «Die Peterskirche». Robert Browning, on the other hand, allowing himself a little poetic licence, succeeded in piercing through the roof and seeing into the church below one soft Christmas night. And so seeing he asked:

«And what is this that rises propped
With pillars of prodigious girth?
Is it really on the earth
This miraculous Dome of God?
Has the angel's measuring rod
Which numbered cubits, gem from gem,
'Twixt the Gates of the New Jerusalem,
Meted it out, – and what he meted
Have the sons of men completed?
– Binding, ever as he bade,
Columns in the colonnade
With arms wide open to embrace
The entry of the human race
To the breast of... what is it, yon building,
Ablaze in front, all paint and gilding
With marble for brick and stones of price
For garniture of the edifice?
Now I see; it is no dream;
It stands there and it does not seem;
For ever, in pictures, thus it looks
Ànd thus have I read of it in books
Often in England, leagues away,
And wondered how these fountains play,
Growing up eternally
Each to a musical water–tree,
Whose blossoms drop, a glittering boon
Before my eyes in the light of the moon,
To the granite lavers underneath».

(ROBERT BROWNING: from «Christmas Eve»)

In the dying days of the old year and the first of the new the Romans, responding to an irrestible, secret summons crowd into the imposing and protective naves of what is, and always has been, their favourite church, Santa Maria in Aracoeli.

Perhaps it is the position of the church, high up on the Capitoline Hill, built on the foundations of other temples to the gods, that of itself provides the appeal. Or perhaps, more simply, it is because one cannot but return at least once a year to the spot where legends, having the ring of truth, soften the otherwise grim succession of events that form two thousand years of history. Where also art and religion triumph in One communal outpouring in the works by the Cosmati mosaic artists, by Benefial, Michelangelo, Bernini, Benozzo, Gozzoli, Pinturicchio, Bregno and Sansovino.

The periodic return to this spot is further heightened by the memory of the great popes, of the celebration of the victory at Lepanto,[1] as can be seen reflected in the emblems that glisten in the gilded ceiling. Beyond all else it remains bound to the spirit of that turbulent Mediaeval Rome which is here found in such a conveniently compendious form. These recollections of great events invite us on those special days to climb once more to the Capitoline summit, slowly savouring and enjoying what were once 124 steps. Nineteen metres wide they are made up of fifteen flights of eight steps each, all fashioned out of marble taken from the great monuments. The entire stairway was completed on 25th October 1348 and stands as a gigantic thanks–offering for Rome's delivery from the black death, as is stated in the Latin epigraph on the façade of the church, a Latin already tainted by the «vulgar tongue» (Italian). The stairway was built by a certain Simone Andreozzi from the Colonna district who was known as «il fabricator de Roma» (evidently a master–craftsman with a reputation for the number of buildings put up in Rome under his direction). The Tribune Cola di Rienzo was the first to climb the steps at the inauguration ceremony. bed the steps.

As one ascends each step one's horizon widens and the view becomes ever richer in detail. Though we may be accused of rhetoric, it cannot be denied that in making the ascent the immense pride of the true Roman is raised to the point where he regards it as the highest manifestation of his, admittedly irascible, nature. Then comes the church itself, what was once the Mediaeval Chamber of the Representatives of the Roman People, together with the monuments, almost bound fast to the walls and together engendering a sense of harmony over the entire site. Every corner conveys an air of the home and the family. As Montaigne remarked «Here everybody feels at home». But from Christmas to Epiphany «the Church of the Senate and People of Rome» is filled by the faithful who pay homage to the celebrated image of the Holy Child who, at the end of the ceremonies, is brought to the head of «the stairway to the sun» and blesses Rome and the world.

In addition to the churches there are the «Madonnelle» (small images of the Virgin Mary), as they were once called, which serve as the visible sign of that particular belief in the Mother of Jesus common in the Roman Catholic world. Set in little shrines the sacred images are placed in the open to keep watch over corners of streets and little piazzas. At one time it was the light of their votive candles on which the Romans had to rely to find their way round the maze of streets, alleys and piazzas. This veneration of the Madonna, it was said in the middle of the last century, is quite spontaneous and genuine among the people of Rome. Go where one will the spot will be consecrated by Her image. It is a form of religious belief that has its roots in an unconscious and complex tradition, often deriving from ancient pagan myths.

In any event hundreds of «Madonnelle» still survive, with their now faded figures, the little light that serves no more, the supporting bracket, the canopy, and the splendid baroque frames. As early as 1853 cavaliere Alessandro Rufini compiled «A List of the Images of the Virgin Mary attached to the outside walls of certain buildings in the Noble City of Rome». These images listed and described in alphabetical order according to the streets and piazzas in which they were to be found and grouped under fourteen districts, came to a total of 1421. To these were added a further 1318 «paintings, bas-reliefs and sculptures of religious subjects». The lights that burnt at night in front of these sacred images numbered 1067.

In these two volumes Rufini also lists objects made of «gold, silver and other materials that adorn the images described». From this we learn that together with the shrines the walls were decorated with the following, which may or may not have been votive–offerings: «316 silver crowns, 920 silver votive hearts, 19 gold ear-rings, 9 silver medallions, 20 various objects in gold and silver, 264 strings of coral, 326 strings of pearls, 20 strings of garnet, 24 different crowns». We see these and other «objects», below or decorating sacred images, in the engravings illustrating the period and its way of life by artists from Thomas to Pinelli. In this regard the second Rufini volume should be mentioned it gives a «list of the votive offerings hung from the images described». This tells us that there were 56 vows painted on plaques, 14 crutches, 9 silk hangings, 10 little dresses for the Virgin, 10 knives, 6 daggers, 2 different weapons, 3 locks of hair». Which makes a total of 110 votive offerings.

[1] The papal fleet's participation in the victory of Lepanto which ended Turkish naval expansion in the Mediterranean.

43

47

48

72

74

# FROM RENAISSANCE TO BAROQUE

Just as Rome has been capable of adapting to every turn of event over the years so it has succeeded today in keeping alive and conserving intact certain features of earlier times and continuing to be enlivened by the spirit of the people, even in the chaos and uproar of a contemporary metropolis. This city, more than any other, lends itself to the merger of diverse external elements. Many of its monuments date from classical times or bear the imprint of the Middle Ages or of the supreme art of the Renaissance, but they are all invariably found in a seventeenth century setting which gives them a baroque framework. They thus present an ambience distinctly eloquent, sumptuous and of a quietly scenic nature, greatly helped by trees, water, flights of steps, columns, obelisks and squares that suddenly open out like shells. Since each view is different from another and every corner holds its element of surprise, Rome should be seen by constantly moving from place to place in order to admire from different vantage points each monument and each site. The top of a tree rising unexpectedly behind a building; a cupola showing above a row of houses, a ruin appearing incongruously amongst modern buildings. The unique beauty of Rome undoubtedly lies in this extreme variety of styles, in the very original accents of its unique character, but also in the alternations of colour which manifest themselves ceaselessly from dawn to dusk. The *lumière* noted by Poussin and Lorenese is explained in the words of Chateaubriand. «A singularly harmonious tone weds the earth, the sky and the water: and thanks to an imperceptible gradation of colours all surfaces seem to join at their extremities so that it is impossible to establish where one shade ends and another begins».

From the highest points in the city, excellent observatories of this poetic world, one may watch the slow transformation of light and colour and observe their quivering currents throughout the day as they dissolve over the cupola of St. Peter's and the smaller cupolas, rather like the submerged triumphal notes of sume huge majestic score. These Renaissance and baroque cupolas, as seen from the Pincian Hill and, to a lesser degree, from other vantage points, have inspired poets and artists of every age from all over the world. They find here a beautiful anthology ready to hand.

A perfect example of light–hearted baroque, the genial baroque of Bernini, is the Fountain of the «Barcaccia» (old barge) at the foot of the Pincian Hill in Piazza di Spagna. Placed sideways on, with its sagging sides, its radiant suns and attachments at either end with which to tow it towards the canals, it is a joke of such exquisite proportions and harmony as to provide a miracle of art. In contrast to this charming caprice there is, not far away, the crashing and thundering of the Trevi Fountain. It was the last of the great baroque fountains, much extolled in poetry and song and closely bound to the Rome of symbolic tradition. One could hardly think of Rome without thinking of the Trevi Fountain. The entire wall of Palazzo Poli has been transformed by Nicola Salvi into a fantasy of statues set among wild rocks and a cascade of water. A triumphal arch applied to a Renaissance palace. The fusion is perfect and the rush and fall of the water adds a dimension of sound to the edifice, in keys of greater or lesser volume, rather like a harmonious organ accompaniment.

This most feclicitous period in the evolution of Rome's art and architecture saw the building of the fountains, whether large or small, simple basins or huge scenic cascades. The period also saw the raising and reinstatement of the obelisks which the Romans had transplanted from Egypt to decorate their monuments and the entrances to mausoleums, and to provide a landmark for their circuses or stadiums. In addition the main streets of the city were straightened, from Via Lungara, which crosses the Tiber, to Via Giulia, the main artery of Renaissance Rome. This was the realization of Julius II's utopian dream the «poetic reordering» of the streets of Rome. These streets are now still voices, at times sorrowful voices, in the more or less contaminated fabric of the city, here and there ruined by ugly modern monstrosities, such as the inescapable view of the colossal hotel on Monte Mario, directly in line with Via Giulia. By way of consolation the street is now lined with antique shops of the highest quality.

Whilst on the subject of streets we must now look at the 1,500 metres of the Corso, the longest and best–known of them.

Stendhal regarded it as «the most beautiful street in the world» and ten years earlier he had spoken of «this most magnificent street, narrow and filled with palaces». It begins in Piazza Venezia, gives the cold shoulder to the Victor Emanuel Monument and runs due north, serving as the boundary line between a number of districts before widening out, with the delicacy and beautiful symmetry of blown glass, into the twin curves of Piazza del Popolo. It then continues on the far side of the Porta del Popolo where it becomes the Via Flaminia leading out of Rome.

The Corso, or Via del Corso as it is now known, is the uncontested queen of Roman streets, not least because it follows traces of the old Roman Via Lata which still exist underground at different levels, thus conferring an absolute supremacy over other roads, however noble they may be. We may therefore speak of the Corso in an absolute sense, indeed as the prototype of all other «corsi». It is the street in which for many years during the carnival season there took place the race of the «barberi» – wild horses let loose without riders from Piazza del Popolo and shortly afterwards recaptured at the foot of the Capitoline Hill A number of harmonious contrasts are to be found in the era that saw the reign of Bernini, Borromini and Pietro da Cortona, as for example the «Pulcin della Minerva», a little obelisk mounted on the back of a Bernini elephant, or the stone flower blossomimg forth from one of the huge Roman baths (taken from the Baths of Caracalla) in front of Palazzo Farnese. Then there is the Triton, that blatant and unreproved exhibitionist sitting against the light bathed in golden threads of water, who continues to flaunt his particularly robust nudity by blowing water skywards and never deigning to look at anyone.

Many of the works of this period became models for the rest of Europe. The graceful design of the river steps at the Porto di Ripetta, unfortunately demolished when the Tiber embankment was built, or the flights of steps and landings of the celebrated Spanish Steps up to Trinità de' Monti, enhanced by the flower stalls and, from time to time, pots of azaleas, and overlooked by the «little red house» where John Keats died. The whole surmounted by the obelisk and the stately twin towers and façade of the church of Trinità de' Monti.

The finest achievement of the Baroque artists in fitting their works into a ground–plan already laid by antiquity is seen in Piazza Navona. Indeed it is said that the most beautiful «picture» of Rome is to be seen from an open window in Palazzo Braschi overlooking the Piazza. It is from there, looking from south to north, that Piazza Navona, especially façades of the houses and in the basins of the fountains, presents a truly magic scene.

«The Circus of Agone is the longest and the most beautiful in Rome», acknowledged François Rabelais. Its supremacy was vaunted with typical Roman insolence in a famous sonnet by Belli. «Se po' fregà Piazza Navona mia / e de San Pietro e de Piazza de Spagna / Cuesta non è una piazza, è una campagna, / un treàto, una fiera, un'allegria». («My Piazza Navona doesn't give a toss for St. Peter's or Piazza di Spagna. This is not a piazza but a countryside, a theatre, a fair, a pleasure ground»). It is nowadays closed to traffic and is visited not only to enjoy the Christmas–Epiphany transformation inherited some decades ago from Piazza St. Eustachio, but also to admire more profoundly the evolutionary cycle of a supreme achievement in urban architectural design which never stales but at each new viewing renews our pleasure and wonder.

The row houses that surround the piazza follow almost exactly the internal perimeter, and to some extent, the external perimeters of the Stadium of Domitian built in A.D. 86. It is not a circus and is therefore without a «spine» (an island running down the middle) or a «finishing line». When rebuilt by Septimius Severus it measured 228 metres by 53 metres on the inside (the future piazza) and 275 by 106 metres on the outside, reaching a height of 18.5 meters by way of 26 steps. After the fall of the Empire the stadium gradually disintegrated, like other classical buildings, into a mass of broken marble, travertine and terracotta and for centuries provided a treasure store for both the rapacious plunderer and the collector of archeological finds. The flattened remains eventually became part of the urban landscape. In 1485 the area was laid with bricks and then in 1588 with paving stones. From the word «agones», meaning gymnastic competitions, it was called successively «Campus agonis», «Agon», «Agones», which gradually became deformed into «Navone» and finally «Navona», referring to its shape which is like that of a ship (nave).

But for many years stadium and piazza coexisted. «Navone, where one jousts and participates in other sports» noted Rucellai during the Jubilee celebrations of 1450, «with steps where the public may sit and watch». Festivals and celebrations have always been the life–blood of the piazza, from the «Lake» to the market, from the Epiphany celebrations to the fortune–tellers, from the most varied cerimonies to the joust of the Saracens, from the Christmas stalls to the hippies. It is all set against a backdrop extolled by painters and engravers alike, from Falda to Piranesi, from Thomas to the sparkling views of Scipione Bonichi.

Bernini, Rainaldi and Borromini had already been commissioned to reinvigorate the piazza, but as well as embellishing the enormous space with works of art on an equally mighty scale (the Fountain of the Four Rivers, for example, in place of a humble, though very useful, drinking trough), they could not let well alone and also built on one side, of the piazza, until then uniform with the opposite side, the monumental church of S. Agnese in Agone (with its concave façade, cupola and belltower). A somewhat incongruous and excessive element to which, however, we have now become accustomed.

117

121

134

# THE RIVER, ITS BRIDGES
# AND THE ISLAND

The Roman region is bisected by the surly and indolent flowing Tiber, with numerous divergencies, rapids, whirlpools and small tributaries dotting its course as well as the large main tributary, the Aniene or so–called Teverone. In the past the river had a deplorable tendency to overflow its banks whenever it was swollen by rain but, despite fears of further flooding in the immediate future, these «excesses» of Father Tiber were diligently recorded on the so–called «tabelle di piena» (high watermark tables). Such tables, engraved on marble tablets with considerable charm (almost making one forget the dramatic reason for their being there), were often decorated with delightful symbols, such as a hand pointing to the level the water had reached on a particular occasion, or a ship sailing on the crest of the flood, together with an appropiate comment inscribed in Latin or the vulgar tongue.

Later, according to precise instructions, some tables were fixed to the Canton della Minerva, on the façade of the church, where they can still be seen, and others to Castel Sant'Angelo and to the Canton della Dogana di Ripa Grande, which has no longer existed for some time. The oldest tablet is to be found under the Arco dei Banchi and dates from 1276 or 1277. Other tablets record further flooding over the years until that disastrous December, following the breaching of Porta Pia (the semi–ritual entry of national troops into the city which finally wrested Rome from the Church and made it part of United Italy) when the little tablets were spread monotonously over the streets and piazzas of half Rome. It was after that fateful year, 1870, that the river was brought under control once and for all by the construction of the providential, if unlovely, embankment. Nevertheless the river remains an essential element of the «poetry» of Rome, as has been illustrated over thousands of years of history.

The city needs the river even if the river, in its turn, could not do without the city. What would the Tiber be, for example, without that monumental «bollard», the only one in the world, represented by Castel Sant'Angelo – without that supreme vantage point for viewing the Tiber where even the current as it passes seems to slow down into little whirlpools of homage? One must also remember a certain statue of the Tiber, clearly of the masculine sex, reclining on a cornucopia and armed with an oar, with the she–wolf and twins beside him. This is the Tiber of myth in that the life of the Romans is said to have begun, in remote and legendary times, with the twins who made their appearance in a basket kept afloat by kindly Father Tiber.

Certainly the Tiber, being the river it is, never was, and never could be what the Thames is to London, the Elbe to Hamburg or the Seine to Paris, that is, a great river port. Also because not even the grandiose and monumental 16th and 17th century buildings flanking the Tiber can mask completely the domestic aspect of the river, its course through the city being confined virtually to the short distance bounded by Ponte Sant'Angelo and Ponte Santa Maria, or Ponte Rotto (the broken Bridge) as it is now called. This aspect of the river could bitterly disappointment the legitimate expectations of anyone seeing it for the first time whose knowledge came from reading the classics. But the ancient Romans thought differently. For them the river was a familiar part of daily life with which they lived in close attachment and whose water, up to the beginning of the century, they drank liberally. It was excellent drinking water in all respects.

We now turn to the bridges, the true Prima Donnas of the Tiber, indifferent even to the matronly presence of the Island of St. Bartholomew, which, among other things, without their help would remain isolated in mid–stream, just where the current is particularly fast and furious. The last bridge to be built was that of the Metropolitana (the new underground line) and seeing it there, spanning the river and looking so frail and delicate, it seems almost an intruder – even if when seen from the embankment at Piazza della Libertà, between trees and flowering bushes growing on banks whose wildness is still untamed, it reminds one of one of Roesler–Franz's paintings. It is worthy of note that this bridge brings up the total number of bridges in the city or immediately outside it to thirty. At the time of the entry into Rome in 1870 they could almost be counted on the fingers of one hand. They were Ponte Milvio, Ponte Sant'Angelo, the iron bridge suspended from the Fiorentini (which cost one «soldino» to cross), Ponte Sisto, the two bridges of the Tiber Island, Cestio and Fabricio and Ponte Rotto, temporarily joined to the two banks by iron girders. Further down river towards the estuary the river was spanned by the Rome–Civitavecchia Railway Bridge which could be opened to allow ships through.

Up to this time bridges were, as a matter of course, named after the districts they served, with the exception of the one named after Pope Sixtus IV. After Unification nationalist enthusiasm produced a rather different nomenclature for the new bridges: Mazzini, Garibaldi, Cavour and Risorgimento, while a further group were named after the House of Savoy: Vittorio Emanuele II, Umberto I, Regina Margherita. The next family to be so honoured were the House of Aosta. Only later was there a return to local names with the new Palatino, Sublicio, Testaccio and Flaminio bridges.

Even now we have not covered them all. There are still the reilway bridges: that of the Rome–North line which can be seem from Monte Antenne and the nearby Tor di Quinto on the Via del Foro Italico, as well as the bridge built for the Roma–Pisa line, just up–stream from the papal Ponte dell'Industria, but now only a road bridge. Again, going down–stream, there are Ponte Marconi, Ponte della Magliana, Ponte di Mezzocamino, Ponte della Scafa. In the sound of the river passing beneath the bridges one fancies one still hears the submerged echo of the life and times and legends of Rome and the Tiber. It is almost as if the surly and yellowish water had overflowed in order to infiltrate centuries of history. And that the bridges marked the stages of that history and halted it, at least for a brief moment, to give pause for memories of past greatness, still in evidence in the archeological remains of all periods to be found on the river bed and its banks.

As we have seen Rome also possesses an island in its stretch of the river, commonly called Isola Tiberina or Isola di San Bartolomeo. In the past it was known variously as Isola di Esculapio, Isola Sacra, Isola Lycaona and even Inter Duos Pontes (Between Two Bridges), as well as Villa dei Languenti (Villa of the Languishing). So many names for one small island, albeit now an indispensable part of the Roman landscape. What would Rome and the Tiber be without this natural feature, much sought after by painters in times past and today and an attractive subject for photographers and film directors. It would be like depriving Paris and the Seine of the l'Île de la Cité and Nôtre Dame. Though much smaller than the large Parisian island, the Isola Tiberina is equally evocative, wrapped as it is in the mists of history and arcane mythology. The physical formation of the island goes back to the time when the Tarquins (from Etruria) were outlawed and the Roman people, in an outburst of hate cut down the corn on the Tarquins' land in Campo Marzio and threw it into the river. The corn piled up on a sand bank just below the Capitoline Hill and the river did the rest, consolidating it with a mass of vegetable matter until such time as the Romans decided to enlarge the island and to make it permanent by artificial means. At a later stage the sides of the island were lined with travertine marble in the shape of a ship in memory of the ship that brought the sacred serpent from Epidaurus. At the same time a temple was erected to Aesculapius, possibly on the same spot on which the church of S. Bartolomeo now stands. At some point the ship's oars were removed and it was «moored» permanently to the two banks of the river by means of the bridges, Cestio and Fabricio, both of which still stand. The first, Ponte Fabricio on the left, is the only ancient Roman bridge to come down to us with its structure almost untouched. Much loved by the Romans for whom the Monastery of the Fatebenefratelli is a homely haven, the island was perhaps even more familiar to them before restorations and enlargements permitted the hospital to occupy, possibly on too large a scale, the whole of the «bows» of the island. There is also a beautiful second church, S. Giovanni Calibita, of great age, facing the other and once the pride and seat of the University of the Molinari. Further there is a tower, Torre dei Caetani, which guards the access to Ponte Quattro Capi and is now occupied in part by a modest but excellent and truly Roman trattoria.

The island has been subject continually, during its long existence, to a thousand dangers, particularly from the two branches of the river that rush past it on either side. The worst of these perils occurred in 1900 when the river was so swollen that it damaged the newly–built embankments. The flood waters breached and brought down a long section of the embankment just up–stream from Ponte Cestio, which gave journalists a field day and delighted early photographers as well as a cameraman who succeeded in filming the event at the very moment it happened. There was great alarm and the usual commission of enquiry was appointed armed with full powers to investigate the cause of the disaster and make proposals to prevent its recurrence. The members duly met in solemn assembly and in due course recommended, among other things, «that the Isola Tiberina be removed to allow the two forks of the river to form a single stream». Even what little remained of Ponte Rotto was to be demolished, possibly «retaining such parts of it as might be considered of historical value». Against this drastic remedy Parliament and people rose in unison and the menace to the island was averted. Only Ponte Sisto still carries the cast–iron reinforcements to widen the carriageway of this harmonious 15th century monument, added in those days of panic caused by technical and socio–political inadequecies. No way has yet been found to restore the bridge to its original lines.

136

REDVX RECEPTA PON
TIFEX FERRARIA
NON ANTE TAM SVPERBI
HVCVSQVE TYBRIDIS
INSANIENTES EXECRA
TVR VORTICES
ANNO DÑI M·D·XOVIII
VIIII·KAL·IANVARII

ANNO DÑI·M·D·XXX
OCTAVO IDVS OCTOBRIS·PONT
VERO SANTISSIMI DÑI
CLEMEN PAPE VII ANNO VII

HVC TIBER ASCENDIT IAMQ
OBRVTA TOTA FVISSET
ROMA·NISI HVC CELEREM
VIRGO TVLISSET OPEM

M·D·LVII·DIE·XI·SEPTEMBRIS
HVC TIMBER ADVENIT·PAVLVS·IIII
QVARTVS·IN·ANNO
TERNO·EIVS·RECTOR·MAXIMVS·
ORBIS·ERAT

144▷

151▷

# LIFE
# IN THE OLDER
# QUARTERS

A first encounter with Rome is not always easy or satisfactory. There exists a certain Roman ornateness arising from events of long ago, such that a traveller on first arriving in the city may find himself experiencing the same feelings of open–eyed wonder that a child feels on first seeing the sea. In the child's case it is a natural phenomenon that provides fascination and the fear; in the visitor's case it is the waves of thousands of years of history, ancient customs, and underlying rhythms. The poets, accustomed as they are to dreaming have, in all epochs, rejoiced on meeting this remarkable «dimension». Byron, as is well known, found in Rome «the city of the soul», and Gogol felt that he had travelled many «verste» (a great distance) nearer to God. But over and above these romantic encounters, Rome conquers everyone by its simpilicity. Stendhal, perspicacious and profound, for many years wrestled with the idea of Rome and the Roman world but without ever allowing it to overwhelm him. Montaigne, himself a «Roman citizen» with wisdom and good taste, was struck by the delightful juxtaposition of two characteristic elements in the Roman landscape (more so in the past than today) roses and artichokes. He likened them to beauty and truth, the spiritual and the material.

Hence, given its boundless scenes and sites, it would be unwise for the visitor to attempt to encompass the city in its entirety. He would be completely submerged by it. To know something of only a fifth part is sufficient to reveal equally clearly the «magnitude» of the metropolis and its background life, to savour the originality of its «quirite»[1] spirit. Just a fifth part would be enough for the interested and cultivated visitor who, dissatisfied with fixed itineraries is prepared to supplement them by following the promptings of his own curiosity and leanings. As soon as he tires of the traffic, which may happen very soon, the visitor is advised to take refuge in one of the pedestrian precincts: Piazza Navona for example has long been restored to that state dreamed of by artists, and a place where all can stroll about at their ease, or there is Piazza Santa Maria in Trastevere which enters with great spirit into the character of that fiercely independent quarter, or Piazza Margana with its open air sculpture exhibitions. In the summer all these squares are unfailingly invaded by the tables and chairs of the trattorias (another place of refuge, even if at a certain price). A little–known pedestrian precinct is Ponte Sant'Angelo, as the stone bollards at each end somewhat peremptorily denote. With the all–pervading presence of the castle, once the mausoleum of Hadrian and transformed by Popes Alexander VI and Leo X, conjuring up thoughts of Tosca and Cavaradossi, the whole benignly watched over by Bernini's Angels of the Passion, with the «sacred» Tiber motionless for a moment below, it is a truly magnificent place to stop and rest. A closely confined plot suspended between sky and river it constitutes a little paradise for fashion models too placed by their photographers against an unquestionably unique backdrop. Wishing to extend one's horizon one has only go to another haven of the pedestrian; Michelangelo's Piazza del Campidoglio, the heart of civic and secular Rome. Other traffic–free areas are those of the main shopping streets such as Via Condotti, Via Frattina, Via della Croce, and Via Borgognona. But a tranquil pause can also be made beside one of the hundreds of splashing fountains, whose murmurings could be quite revealing if we are to believe Jean Cocteau. «The Roman fountains», he wrote, «let fall whatever they are thinking, while the (Fascist) regime bids them keep silent». Many foreigners prefer to see Rome on foot so as to enjoy it «en flanant» as the Parisians would say. They are inclined suddenly to pop out of alleys and squares, in pairs or in parties, certain of making new discoveries and then having the pleasure of telling their friends about them. This is an excellent means of exploration and dissemination, and succeeds in bringing the hidden beauties of the city into direct touch with the sensibility and taste of everyone. At Ferragosto (the traditional summer holiday), when virtually all Romans leave the city, it is the visitors who then become masters of a city more sharply defined, of rediscovered vistas, and of roads more or less free of traffic.

Seen from above on market days Campo de' Fiori looks like a multico-loured collage of stalls and umbrellas, good–naturedly using as their centre–piece the bronze statue of Giordano Bruno, that misunderstood martyr. «Here it was that the flames devoured him». This lively market square still governs the life of the district, and continues to irradiate vitality as it has been accustomed to do so ever since the 15th century when Rome finally threw off its medieval vestments. At that time it was a centre of trade and the headquarters of the nascent art of print-ing, and was filled with wine–shops, inns and taverns. But it was also called the «cursed square». Hangings, torturings and burnings all took place here. Giordano Bruno was one of the victims, and the «Terrina» (the Tureen) later moved to the Chiesa Nuova, seems to mock the justice of the inquisition with its admonitory inscription, «Ama Dio e non fallire, fa del bene e lassa dire». («Love God and never fail to do so, do good and leave it at that»). There followed a decline in the square's importance in the 18th century as new centres and meeting places sprang up elsewhere and it was not until 1889 that the new «Italian» Rome remembered its maligned philosopher by erec-ting a statue to him, amidst much bitter debate and differences of opinion that went on for years. But it must be said that this statue by Ettore Ferrari has since become a much loved and indispensable part of the piazza. Indeed in the afternoons when the market is closed and the refuse cleaned away, the philosopher figures as the pensive umpire of impromptu football matches, which for years have been played there by the rowdy boys of this still surviving part of an older Rome. In winter the young people go so far as to light fires at the foot of the statue, treating it like a totem, while from time to time, regrettably, from the adjoining streets come the shrieks of those who have suffered a «scippo» (had their handbags snatched). All around the square, still within the Campo de' Fiori quarter, there exists a so–called «vanished Rome», which fortunately has not vanished at all, as in Via dei Cappellari where there is an arch joining the upper floors of the houses on each side of the narrow street, in one of which Pietro Trapassi, called Metastasio, was born. It is a street very dear to painters–perhaps too much so.

In the nearby Via del Pellegrino there is an arch (Arco degli Acetari) which looks onto a very rare scene of intimate city life as it was lived many decades ago. It was once common in the Ghetto and elsewhere but is now almost completely vanished. Few people, even Romans, know of this priceless corner of the city but film directors jump at the chance of shooting a scene in such a perfect location. From there, going back to Campo de' Fiori and cutting through from Piazza Farnese to Capo di Ferro we arrive at the end of the Via Giulia. Then, crossing the river by means of the Ponte Sisto we reach the part known as Trastevere («across the Tiber»). A district whose flag continues to carry the head of a roaring lion on a red field, a sign of the immutability of its borders and its traditions, even though enquiries into that world and its inhabitants go on ceaselessly veering between praise and alarm. The «Trasteverini», as they are called, are a people apparently without inhibitions and vaunting a spirit of liberty, as expressed over the centuries in many different ways. This is the quarter of Titta degli Anguillara who refused to bare her head even before Charles V; of Giuditta Tavani Arquati, a symbol of female heroism, who was martyred in defence of the ideal of patriotism. A quarter which more than any other bore the brunt of the siege during the Roman Republic of 1849. Even when the French eventually occupied the city no «Trasteverino» dreamt of giving up his knife, holding the firm conviction, backed by the lessons of history, that no man worthy of the name would ever be separated from his blade. This then was Trastevere and these her people who still today maintain their fierce pride. They know when to remain silent but, when they do speak, reveal a freedom of expression and a colourful and effective use of dialect. They are renowned for their loyalty and have fought hard, above all with their own natures, to cope with the manifold ills of modern urban development. It was once a thriving port at a time when the river was the principle means of transport and communication. Vessels came twenty-four miles up–stream from the river mouth at Fiumicino and moored at the wharves known as the Ripa Grande. The port, once so active, disappeared with the construction of the embankments which, while finally protecting the city from floods, reduced the Tiber of history and myth to a characterless canal.

Whoever wishes to really «see» Trastevere today, to feel the «living» Trastevere, disregarding both ancient fables and modern analysis, must direct his steps towards other goals: lose himself in the streets, visit the churches when the sun glows through the high windows (S. Maria in Trastevere, S. Cecilia, S. Maria dell'Orto, S. Giovanni Battista dei Genovesi), stand in the evening in one of those passageways in which are found the trattorias and taverns so much frequented by the Romans. It is pointless to claim that one is in a quarter that is mostly «secret» (some say it should be «forbidden») which has to be «discovered» by attempting to adopt the local psychology and follow a clearly perceptible course, in order not to disturb an atmosphere that has reigned over Trastevere for centuries and thus makes it «different».

After visiting the art treasures it will be found equally inspiring to make a stop in that kind of «umbilicus» of Trastevere, Piazza de' Renzi, named after an ancient family that lived there. It is not easy to find without a good map as Via del Moro or Vicolo dei Cinque (both names given for good reasons) which one traverses when coming from Ponte Sisto succeed in missing the square completely. One must remember to turn into Via del Cipresso or Vicolo de' Renzi and then one will find oneself suddenly in the tiny square. A square so authentic that not even a director with all his artistry and theatrical props could render it more truly itself, more unexpectedly real.

[1] Quirite: historical term for a Roman citizen.

155

173

174

189

1  View of the picturesque Ponte Nomentano, over the river Aniene, this bridge was frequently depicted by 17th and 18th century artists.

2  The ruins of Villa dei Quintilli (4th century), among the most grandiose remains found in the Roman Campagna, near the Old Appian Way.

3  A characteristic Roman «In Memorium», one of the many monuments to the dead standing along the Via Appia; the most beautiful and most important of the consular roads.

4-5  The Claudian acqueduct, named after its architect and built in 312 B.C. The sequence of identical arches of the Acqueducts in the region of the Via Appia give this part of the Roman Campagna its unique character.

6-7  The towers of the Circo di Massenzio, built in 309, and the tomb of Cecilia Metella, whose cylindrical mausoleum (with a diameter of 20 metres) dates from the last decades of the Republic.

8  A sheperd and his flock with ruins in the background – a surviving view of an older pastoral Lazio.

9  A stretch of the Via Appia showing grooves in the original paving stones made by ancient wheels.

10  Roman Colombarium (dove–cote) near the tomb of the Scipioni family between Porta S. Sebastiano and Porta Latina.

11  View of the Appia Antica near the «Casal Rotondo», an ancient tomb of the Republican era, and next to it a brick wall bearing decorative marble fragments of masks and inscriptions.

12  Triumphal arch attributed to Druso, at the end of the Via di Porta S. Sebastiano, just before Porta S. Sebastiano.

13  Sheep grazing in the so-called «Valley of Hell» below St. Peter's.

14  The towers of the ancient Porta Asinaria seen against the pediment of the Lateran Basilica.

15  The Pyramid of Caius Cestius near Porta S. Paolo.

16  The Roman Forum, centre of life in the ancient city, brought to light only during the last century.

17  The Forum and the slope of the Palatine Hill seen through the Arch of Septimius Severus.

18  The Roman Forum; columns of the Temple of Castor and Pollux and the Arch of Titus.

19  The spring of the goddess Giuturna in the Forum. According to legend Castor and Pollux watered their horses here after their arrival in Rome with news of victory over the Latins (496 B.C.).

20  The Trajan market crescent and the ancient Via Biberatica. The cats, permanent residents, following the «gattara» whose turn it is to feed them.

21  Flagstones of the Sacred Way and marble inscriptions in the Forum, with the Palatine in the background.

22  The Colosseum and the attic storey of the Arch of Constantine seen from the Palatine hill.

52 In the portico of S. Maria in Cosmedin we see the ancient tombstone which gives the whole area its name: Bocca della Verità. According to legend if a perjuror should be so unwise as to put his hand into the mouth it would be bitten off.

53 Interior of S. Maria in Cosmedin, the splendour of the mosaic work by the Cosmati artists contrasting with the free and simple lines of the church.

54-55 The church of S. Prassede. Detail of the mosaics (9th. century) in the chapel of S. Zenone. This is the most important Byzantine monument in Rome, called «The Garden of Paradise» because of its evocative beauty. «The Pillar of the Flagellation», which was brought from Jerusalem in 1223, is preserved in a little room nearby.

56-57 S. Pietro in Montorio on the Janiculum and the little chapels on the Via Crucis that go up from Trastevere to the square in front of the church. This is where St. Peter is said to have been crucified.

58-59 The Church of S. Onofrio which occupies another strategic point on the Janiculum. To this monastery, with cloisters on two levels decorated by cavalier d'Arpino with frescoes depicting the life of St. Onophrius, Torquato Tasso came to die and is buried in the church.

60 Ss. Quattro Coronati, a fortified church in an isolated position near the Colosseum, contains this jewel of a cloister built in the 13th century.

61 La Via Crucis – with the stations of the cross – on the street leading from the Arch of Titus in the Forum to the little church of S. Bonaventura on the Palatine.

62 Against the background of the Renaissance portico of S. Maria in Dominica, on the Coelian Hill, stands the famous «Navicella», almost certainly a votive offering of Roman origin.

63 Picturesque medieval buttresses of the Clivio di Scauro to the left of the church of Ss. Giovanni e Paolo. (Clivio: rise or hillock).

64 The cupola of S. Andrea della Valle, second only in size to St. Peter's.

65 Via di S. Paolo della Croce with the cupola and campanile of Ss. Giovanni e Paolo.

66 Representation in bronze of a dream of St. Francis (in which he was supporting the Lateran Basilica, in danger of falling) facing the Basilica of S. Giovanni in Laterano «the mother of all the churches».

67-68-69 St. Paul's Without the Walls or Basilica Ostiense, the largest in Rome after St. Peter's, whose grandiose interior – reminiscent of the Roman imperial basilicas – is divided into five naves by eighty monolithic columns of granite. The apse is decorated with a large mosaic of Christ giving a blessing. The huge paschal candelabra, made by Nicolò di Angelo and Pietro Vassalletto in the 12th century, is 5.60 metres tall and shows scenes from Christ's Passion alternating with a decoration of animals, chimera and entwined vegetation.

70-71 The facade of Trinità dei Monti crowning the famous Spanish Steps. The little door of the convent beside it gives onto a remarkable view of the cupola of S. Carlo al Corso with the cupola of St. Peter's in the distance.

72 Shrines to the Madonna in Piazza della Pigna, taken from Vicolo delle Ceste.

73 The baroque façade of S. Maria della Pace, by Pietro da Cortona.

74 Shrine at the corner of Palazzo Ricci in the Square of the same name, seemingly in conversation with the monochromes decorating the facade.

75 Religious fresco above the door of the Convento delle Oblate a Tor de' Specchi, in Via del Teatro di Marcello.

an attractive fountain by Giacomo della Porta (1578) upon which the Egyptian obelisk was erected in 1711.

110-111     Via Giulia: a classical straight stretch of about a kilometre in length dating from the Renaissance. It is lined with beautiful palaces and churches where one can see works by Bramante, Raphael, Bernini and Fuga. At one end towards Ponte Sisto we find the Fontana del Mascherone, crowned with the Farnese lily.

112     Via Giulia. An 18th century painting of the nave of St. Peter's in the window of one the numerous elegant antique shops in this street.

113     The «Pulcin della Minerva», a little stone elephant designed by Bernini supporting an Egyptian obelisk dating from the 6th century B.C.

114-115     Peaceful Piazza Farnese, dominated by the façade of the 16th. century Palazzo Farnese, a masterpiece by Sangallo and Michelangelo. In the square stand twin fountains from which water gushes up from huge Farnese lilies and then falls into the colossal Egyptian granite bathtubs taken from the Baths of Caracalla.

116     The elegant facade of the Palazzo Spada in Piazza Capo di Ferro, decorated with scrolls and freizes and statues by Mazzoni.

117-118     The walls and ceilings of the Galleria degli Stucchi in Palazzo Spada, built in about 1540 by Giulio Merisi da Caravaggio for cardinal Girolamo Capo di Ferro. For some time it has been the seat of the Consiglio di Stato.

119     Roman courtyards. A lively wrought–iton gate, the decoration inspired by grape–vines.

120     A courtyard in Via del Gesù decorated with an arrangement of classical sculptures, and a water–clock that still works, designed by father Domenico Embriaco who also designed the more famous water–clock on the Pincian Hill.

121     The so–called «Bath of Venus», a splendid nympheum in the courtyard of Palazzo Borghese.

122     Villa Doria Pamphili, outside Porta S. Pancrazio, is the largest park in Rome. Designed by Algardi (1650) it is full of fountains, statues and cascades.

123     The large fountain in Piazza S. Maria in Trastevere, in the heart of the oldest part of the quarter, was designed by Carlo Fontana (1692).

124     The huge mask on the fountain in Piazza Pietro d'Illiria on the Aventine Hill. This mask once adorned a fountain at Porto Leonino on the right bank of the Tiber in front of Palazzo Salviati.

125     The Fontana delle Tartarughe (Tortoises) a work of «Tuscan» delicacy in this very Roman quarter. Built by Taddeo Landini in 1585 from a design by Giacomo della Porta.

126-127-128-129-130-131     Piazza Navona: one of the largest and most delightfull baroque squares in Rome. Bounded by the buildings that rose up on the remains of Domitian's Stadium, and dominated by the Fountain of the Four Rivers in the centre, a fanciful work by Bernini, crowned by a tall obelisk, in front of which stands the splendid Borromini façade of the church of S. Agnese. There are two other fountains: the «Moro» opposite Palazzo Pamphili, taking its name from the central figure fighting a dolphin, sculpted in 1655 from a design by Bernini, and at the opposite end of the square the Fontana del Nettuno, built in the 19th. century and representing Neptune struggling with an octopus. Used for centuries as a jousting ground and for various sports, races and games, Piazza Navona is now one of the best loved and most popular places with the Romans.

132-133-134     Piazza Navona at Christmas time, with its traditional market stalls where toys and sweetmeats remain on sale until Epiphany Sunday.

135 Seagulls over a swollen Tiber.

136 The parapet of Ponte Sisto, the «Fontanone» and the slopes of the Janiculum seen through a lacework of plane trees lining the banks of the river Tiber.

137 A «Fiumarola» or «Tiber–boat», in the background Ponte Sant'Angelo and St. Peter's.

138-139-140-141 Ponte Sisto with its harmonious series of 15th. century arches was the only bridge built by the popes after those built during the Empire. Crossing the bridge on the way to Trastevere one has a splendid view of the Janiculum and the «Fontanone» di Ponte Sisto. The latter is a large fountain in the shape of a shrine designed by G. Fontana in 1612, first erected in Via Giulia and then transported here in 1898.

142 «The Tiber reached here»: historic tablets on the façade of S. Maria sopra Minerva dating from past centuries when there were frequent floods; similar tablets may be seen in many other corners of Rome.

143 Built in 62 B.C. to join the island to the left bank of the Tiber, Ponte Fabricio is the oldest bridge in Rome and is still practically in its original state even now.

144 The remains of Ponte Rotto, or the Broken Bridge, built by Gregory XIII on the ruins of the Roman Ponte Emilio. Behind is the southern end of the Isola Tiberina and its connecting bridges, Ponte Cestio and Ponte Fabricio.

145 Ponte Fabricio, called locally the Ponte dei Quattro Capi (Bridge of the Four Heads) after the two quadrifaced heads on the parapet of the bridge.

146-147-148 View of the Isola Tiberina and Ponte Fabricio with the medieval Torre dei Caetani, all that remains of the old castle.

149 The Baroque facade of S. Bartolomeo de Insula, overshadowed by the Romanesque campanile. In this picturesque little square stands a 19th century memorial to four saints.

150 Ponte Cestio, re–built in the 19th century with materials from the original bridge built in 46 B.C. by L. Cestio and later restored during the Empire. This bridge joins the island to the right bank of the Tiber.

151 Above the island and the bridges rise the cupolas of S. Carlo ai Catinari and S. Andrea della Valle, competing with each other on the Roman skyline.

152-153-154 Medieval alleyways and houses in Trastevere that give this district its particular character. (Trastevere or «Across the Tiber», the district of Rome on the opposite bank from the ancient city).

155 The knife–grinder has replaced his traditional cart with a bycicle, but this type of local service continues.

156 Piazza Santa Maria in Trastevere, one of the corners of Rome that has remained more or less unchanged. The Basilica is the oldest to have been dedicated the Virgin Mary and was built in the 12th century, its facade is richly decorated with mosaics and a Romanesque campanile.

157-158-159-160 A peaceful village life can even be found in the heart of a great city. This is one of the most attractive aspects of this quarter, one which so many foreigners have enjoyed to advantage.

161 In summertime the central square in Trastevere is filled with restaurant tables.

162 A shrine in Via Uffici del Vicario, complete with lamp and canopy.

163-164 The little market in Via della Pace near Piazza Navona.

202 The Fontana del Facchino, in Via Lata represents a real person – a water–vendor whose name and surname is known. This is one of the «talking» statues of Rome (see also fig. 194). Together with the Pasquino, Marforio, Madama Lucrezia and the Abbot Luigi, he is a member of the «congresso degli arguti» – the «congress of the sharp – witted».

Layout: Giancarlo Gasponi - Rouhyeh Avaregan
Colour separations: NEWSELE - MILANO
Filmset: Linotipia LIFE - TRENTO
Printing: PRINTERS - TRENTO
Printed in Italy - 1985   ISBN 3-87051-389-6